MULTUM IN PARVO

MULTUM IN PARVO

AN ESSAY IN

POETIC IMAGINATION

BY

CARL ZIGROSSER

GEORGE BRAZILLER · NEW YORK

TO LESSING J. ROSENWALD

A NOTE OF ACKNOWLEDGMENT

The following quotations are incorporated in the text by the kind permission of the author or publisher: the description of the ideograph *Yung* by Hugh Gordon Porteus, from his *Background of Chinese Art* (Faber and Faber, London, 1937); the translation (with commentary) of a *haiku* by Harold G. Henderson from his *Introduction to Haiku* (Doubleday and Co., N.Y., 1958); and the poem *The Kitten* by Ogden Nash (Little, Brown and Co., Boston). The Greek quotations are taken from the respective volumes of the *Loeb Classical Library*.

The cluster of acorns and oak leaves used as a background on the dust jacket is taken from a stipple engraving by Legrand after Gerard van Spaendonck, in the collection of the Philadelphia Museum of Art.

LIST OF ILLUSTRATIONS

All except the first are reproduced in the original dimensions

PLATE I
CHIANG YEE (Chinese, contemporary)
YUNG (Chinese ideograph for Eternity),
brush and ink drawing, Carl Zigrosser Collection.

PLATE 2
PEREGRINO DA CESENA (Italian, fl. ca. 1500–1525)
ORPHEUS, engraving, Kupferstich Kabinett,
Berlin-Dahlem.

PLATE 3
ADAM ELSHEIMER (German, 1578–1610)
NYMPH DANCING WITH A TAMBOURINE,
etching, Hind No. 9, Philadelphia Museum of Art,
Academy Collection.

PLATE 4
WILLIAM BLAKE (English, 1757–1827)
SABRINA'S SILVERY FLOOD, woodcut,
trial proof from the unmutilated block
for Thornton's *Eclogues of Virgil*, 1821,
National Gallery of Art, Washington, D.C.,
Lessing J. Rosenwald Collection.

[7]

PLATE 5

EDWARD CALVERT (English, 1799–1883)
CHAMBER IDYLL, wood engraving, 1831,
Finberg No. 10, first state before the inscription and date
were removed.

PLATE 6

HANS HOLBEIN (German, ca. 1497–1543)
DEATH AND THE VIRGIN, woodcut,
engraved by Hans Lützelberger, from *Les Simulachres
... de la Mort*, Lyon, 1538, first edition,
Library of Congress, Washington, D.C.,
Lessing J. Rosenwald Collection.

PLATE 7

ALBRECHT ALTDORFER (German, ca. 1480–1538)
AGONY IN THE GARDEN, woodcut,
from the set of the *Fall and Redemption of Man*,
ca. 1515, Bartsch No. 19.

PLATE 8

JOHN J. A. MURPHY (American, contemporary)
ADORATION OF THE SHEPHERDS,
wood engraving, 1920, Philadelphia Museum of Art.

PLATE 9

JACQUES CALLOT (French, 1592–1635)
THE LAST SUPPER, etching, from the set of *La Petite
Passion*, 1624, Lieure No. 538, first state.

[8]

PLATE 10
REMBRANDT VAN RIJN (Dutch, 1606–1669)
THE GOLDSMITH, etching, 1655, Hind No. 285,
first state, Philadelphia Museum of Art, Academy Collection.

PLATE 11
CHARLES NICOLAS COCHIN (French, 1715–1790)
PARADE, etching, 1759, Jombert No. 249,
Philadelphia Museum of Art.

PLATE 12
THOMAS BEWICK (English, 1753–1828)
WOMAN HANGING OUT CLOTHES,
wood engraving, from *The History of British Birds*,
second edition, 1805, Beinecke Library, Yale University.

PLATE 13
FRANCISCO GOYA (Spanish, 1746–1828)
THE PRISONER, etching, Delteil No. 31,
second state of three, Worcester Art Museum.

PLATE 14
MAX WEBER (American, 1881–1961)
MOTHER AND CHILD, woodcut, ca. 1918,
Joseph Blumenthal Collection.

PLATE 15
ROCKWELL KENT (American, contemporary)
AIR MAIL STAMP, wood engraving, 1932,
Philadelphia Museum of Art.

MULTUM
IN
PARVO

THE phrase *multum in parvo* has always had a special significance for me. In its terse and compact Latin diction, it exemplifies exactly what it connotes: much in little. The archetype of brevity, however, is not easy to define. Abstraction, conciseness, symbolism, and imaginative potential are basic in the concept. A multiplicity of detail is concentrated into a unified principle, the particular is transformed into the universal, a largeness of meaning is conveyed with the utmost economy of means. This largeness of meaning should be accompanied by a dramatic impact, in a word: insight with a gasp.

Where are prime examples of multum in parvo to be found? Not generally in the realm of sound or music, for the sequence of time is an integral ingredient in our perception of music, one note after another producing the pattern of form. Compression is possible only where perception is immediate or nearly so. The appreciation of form through touch likewise involves a time factor. As far as other senses are concerned, those of taste and smell have never been sufficiently developed in man to admit of pointed brevity. At best, the emotive stimulus of taste and smell is gained by association. No, the happy hunting ground for multum in parvo is through the eye and mind, among mathematical formulae and symbols, in the concise and epigrammatic forms of poetry, and in the miniature forms of visual art. Furthermore, from a purist's point of view, neither a fragment of a longer poem nor a detail of a picture can be accepted strictly as multum in parvo.

Mathematical equations obviously meet the required standard for abstraction, even though their emotional impact is limited to relatively few people. There is nothing more awe-inspiring than the macrocosmic conciseness of Einstein's equation $E = mc^2$. Most of the equations of mathematics or physics do have a certain muchness in them, but not all are so simple, basic, or elegant. The difficulty in connection with such formulae is that they may be universal in application but not universal in comprehension. One must be a specialist and learn a special language to understand them. Multum in parvo should be potentially accessible to all mankind.

More universal of comprehension, though limited to the Oriental world, are the ideographs and verse forms of

China and Japan. The graphic symbol of the ideograph, each form standing for an idea, is, in essence, much in little; and, likewise, the very syntax of Oriental thought requires, indeed depends upon, imagination to bind the symbols into a comprehensible phrase or sentence. The Chinese ideograph for "eternal," *yung* (here delineated by Chiang Yee, Plate 1), might well serve as a paradigm for multum in parvo. We discover that it is made up of eight basic strokes. It happens that with these eight basic strokes nearly all Chinese characters can be written—an infinitude of means as well as of meaning. But there is more to the symbol than an exercise in permutations and combinations: there are also the calligraphic elements, the sensuous action of the brush and the spirit that motivates it. The direction, the tension or tenderness of the stroke, the vitality of the movement, and the conscious design of the whole have a direct appeal to the imagination, and create an image of enduring beauty and significance. Much has been written about this ideograph; and the Eight Laws of Writing were codified in the T'ang dynasty on the basis of this single character. Hugh Gordon Porteus has written a description of the brush strokes as they are made. Because it reveals so much of Chinese style, and because it gives such a vivid if personal account of action painting, I shall quote it here:

> The first stroke is the slanting dot (at the top) which must
> be started with the brush moving to the right, with gradu-

ally increasing pressure, and finished with a grinding veer
to the left. The second stroke is the short horizontal line
(below it) drawn with a "bridling" movement from left
to right, and finished with a half revolution of the brush
which is thereby prepared for the downward motion of
the third or perpendicular stroke, drawn with the brush
turned half left and finishing with a "crouching" gesture
ready for the short sudden spring upwards of the fourth
stroke, the upward hook. These four strokes are to be
written with force but comparatively slowly. The re-
maining strokes are swifter, and in the nature of stabs.
The fifth stroke is the upward spike (on the left) executed
with a whipping movement, like a backhand cut, with
power in reserve at the end, ready for the sweeping or
"skimming" thrust of the descending sixth stroke (also on
the left). The seventh stroke, on the right-hand side of the
perpendicular, has the staccato quality of the sudden peck
of a bird. The brush starts (from right to left) at the thick
head of the stroke with a twisting motion, descending like
a bird with grace. The eighth (and most difficult) final
stroke plunges downwards to the right with a "tearing"
force, gradually braked and broadened, like a person or a
vehicle "pulling up" and with a gesture of "looking back."
These are, roughly described, the Eight Laws of Yung on
which the art of brush calligraphy is based.

I have spoken of the terse syntax of Oriental thought, in
which imagination is a necessary ingredient. In addition,
the Chinese, and especially the Japanese, have been partial
to concise verse forms. There is for example the Japanese

haiku, a poem of seventeen syllables (three lines of five, seven, five). Bashō Matsuo (1644–1694) is generally considered to have developed the form from a kind of linked verse found in Chinese and Japanese. Here is his first poem in the new style (1679) and one of the most famous, in Harold G. Henderson's translation and commentary:

On a withered branch	Kare-eda ni
a crow has settled—	karasu-no tomari
autumn nightfall.	aki-no-kure

There are at least two points of technique which make it a model. First, the over-all mood or emotion is produced by a simple description, a plain statement of fact which makes a picture. Second, the two parts that make up the whole are compared to each other, not in simile or metaphor, but as two phenomena, each of which exists in its own right. This may be called "the principle of internal comparison" in which the differences are just as important as the likenesses. Here it is not simply that "over the withered landscape the autumn nightfall settles like a crow." It is also the contrast of the small black body of the crow with the vast amorphous darkness of the nightfall—and whatever else the reader may find in it. It is easy to see how the use of this technique helps to give depth to *haiku*, and to make them starting points for thought and imagination.

Here is another *haiku*, in a more subjective and personal tone, by Issa (1763–1828), written at the death of his only surviving child.

[15]

The dewdrop world	Tsuyu-no-yo wa
may be a world of dew—	tsuyu-no-yo nagara
and yet—and yet	Sari nagara

The translation is based on those by R. H. Blyth, Donald Keene, and Harold G. Henderson. In Buddhist scripture, the evanescence and transitoriness of our conditioned world is likened to a dewdrop, a cloud, or a dream. In his anguish, the poet finds little consolation in the tenets of the Pure Land Sect and the promised splendors of Buddha Amida's Western Paradise.

There are no verse forms in Occidental literature comparable to *haiku* or the similar but more satirical *senryu*. In classical poetry how concise can one be and still be able to kindle emotional response? Do the so-called Homeric epithets fit into the category of multum in parvo? Such as, for instance:

παρα θινα πολυφλοισβοιο θαλασσης

"by the shore of the much sounding sea," with onomatopoeia in its suggestion of the thunder and hiss of the surf. It certainly projects an image of nature with great economy of means; yet the emotional potential is relatively meager because of its limited reference and fragmentary nature. One must turn to the lyric for emotive impact, Sappho's, for example, with its utterly simple imagery and chiseled perfection:

Δεδυκε μεν ἁ σελαννα
και Πληιαδες μεσαι δε
νυκτες παρα δ᾽ἐρχετ᾽ ὠρα
ἐγω δε μονα κατευδο

The moon has set,
And the Pleiades.
In the mid of night,
Each hour comes and goes,
And I lie alone.

Not all lyrics can be rated as multum in parvo, for many of them lack the quality of conciseness. There is no fixed form to the lyric: it can be long or short, a single unit or a series of stanzas. The epigram is a more likely form, since it is pointed and terse, and makes up in wit and dramatic impetus what it may lack in emotional overtones. But, again, not all epigrams are memorable. One of my favorites is preserved in the eleventh book of the Greek Anthology. Never has the life and achievement of an incompetent portrait painter and a miserable man been summed up more devastatingly than by Lucilius in two lines:

Εἰκοσι γεννησας ὁ ζωγραφος Εὐτυχος υἱους
οὐδ᾽ απο των τεκνον οὐδεν ὁμοιον ἐχει

The painter Eutychos begot twenty sons,
But not even among his children did he get a likeness.

Here is another epigram from the anonymity of mediaeval Latin:

[17]

> Mel in ore, verba lactis,
> Fel in corde, fraus in factis.

> Honey in the mouth, words of milk,
> Gall in the heart, fraud in deeds.

It is a precise and concise portrait of a hypocritical evildoer. The imagery has a fresh pertinence, and is cast in a form both elegant and ingenious. The mellifluous sound of the first line stands in contrast to the harshness of the second, with its emphatic f alliteration and the dissonant note of the fr combination. The two lines are neatly tied together by the parallelism of Mel in ore : Fel in corde. The epigram dates from the period when classical Latin, based upon quantitative rhythm, had been changed into mediaeval Latin, employing such devices as accented beat, rhyme, and alliteration.

There is a great temptation to continue citing examples of multum in parvo from the Greek Anthology, from collections of *haiku*, and from the works of Martial, Goethe, Mörike, Edward Fitzgerald, Emily Dickinson, the Imagists, to name only a few. I shall yield only once more to offer Ogden Nash's amusing but profound quatrain:

> The trouble with a kitten is
> That
> Eventually it becomes a
> Cat.

It might be more pertinent and rewarding, now, to turn

to another art, and review what forms the idea of multum in parvo assumes in painting and graphic art. Many paintings in miniature exist; but they are mostly portrait miniatures or illuminations in mediaeval manuscripts, and do not have the universality or accessibility desirable for the genus. The media of printmaking, namely etching or engraving on copper or wood, provide a more fertile field, and possess the same universal accessibility that is inherent in a printed page of literature. But here, unlike the noumenal world, we are confronted with tangible dimensions. The size is tiny and the concept big—much in little. The very disparity between large and small makes for tension and concentration. The area is small enough to be perceived by a single glance; layer after layer of the meaning unfolds within it. The burden of the appeal is carried by the message; the execution may be that of a virtuoso, but must always be subordinate to the desired end.

Message and meaning are not very fashionable, nowadays, as applied to art, and particularly to painting; but they do have their place in fine prints as part of the basic tradition of graphic art. The concept of multum in parvo, however, might well stand as a salutary influence in counteracting the vogue for huge, relatively empty canvases and bravura techniques. Modern painting, without question, can be an exciting adventure, largely because of the stimulus to the imagination in the use of ambiguous imagery. The painter, in this instance both allusive and elusive, works on the beholder's feelings by adumbration. But insofar as modern painters emphasize execution at the expense of any significant content, they may ultimately find themselves traveling on a dead-end road. The affective potentialities of technique are limited and sooner or later exhausted, whereas those of human nature are infinite in their variety. The themes derived from mankind and its concerns have never failed as a basic source of inspiration. They are provocative of countless variations and reflections on man's condition. Because they are based upon a common heritage, the artist using them can count on the imaginative response of the beholder also. That response, however, will be personal and vary with the individual. Each man makes his own testament. When, therefore, I cite prints as instances of much in little, my choice and justification will necessarily be subjective. In their interpretation, they will merely be examples of what prints mean to me.

First of all, I would like to exhibit two little prints slanted toward the pagan world. The first is *Orpheus*, a copper engraving in niello style, by Peregrino da Cesena (Plate 2) in the first quarter of the sixteenth century. It is an ornament print, and may have served as a model for a wood carver, an intarsia worker, or a wall decorator. But it is more than a run-of-mill tool or model for a craftsman. There is a certain inwardness and mystery in the portrayal of Orpheus playing to the animals, a suggestion of the magic, the power, and the charm of music. The spirit of the Renaissance is in this little print, the youthful joyous wonder, the exhilaration of the discovery of an ancient pagan world. The gods of the ancient world seemed closer and more real in those days.

The etching by Adam Elsheimer (Plate 3) in the seventeenth century is likewise a glimpse of an ancient or forgotten world. It is more free in execution, more painterly than Peregrino's engraving, for Elsheimer was primarily a painter who only occasionally made an etching, quickly extemporized out of the inspiration of the moment. Many of his works, even his paintings, are small in size, concentrated and intense. A German by birth, he lived much of his life in Italy. Unworldly, unsuccessful, he died in a debtor's prison. He was a painter's painter: both Rembrandt and Rubens cherished his work and owned paintings by him. He lived in the world of imagination, and saw sights not visible to ordinary folk, the demigods of the fields and forests, Pan, the nymphs and fauns, who still live furtively and half-forgotten in out-of-the-way places. Not many people have the gift of second sight, children perhaps, and some poets and artists, Picasso in our time, or H. W. Nevinson and James Stephens. In Elsheimer's etching, *Nymph Dancing with a Tambourine*, the lines, for all their casual waywardness, weave a magic spell; and the figures of the nymphs and fauns tingle with life.

The shaggy gods and rural divinities were not the only inhabitants of Arcadia: there were also the rustics who tilled the fields and the herdsmen who tended their flocks, piping the while in true bucolic fashion. Thus is myth scaled down to human terms, and Arcadia becomes not so much a place, as the locus of our dreams and longings, the Golden Age, the Land of Cockayne, Île de Cythère, the Rock Candy Mountains. The pastoral life was plain and simple, and closely attuned to Nature. The idea therefore can have a deep and special meaning for us in our troubled and complex world, even as it had for our forebears. The phrase *Et in Arcadia ego*, "I too dwelt (or was born) in Arcadia," has haunted the imagination of mankind for centuries. It was the theme of Poussin's noble painting in the Louvre, where the shepherds are spelling out the inscription on the tombstone. Goethe used it as the motto of his book, *Italienische Reise*. And even in the works of the very writers who originally celebrated Arcadia and the bucolic life, Theocritus, Longus, Virgil, and the others, one senses more of wishful fantasy than of realistic observation. Of all idylls, whether literary or visual, those cut in wood by William Blake will always retain their high place in our regard. They were commissioned as illustrations to an imitation of Virgil's First Eclogue by a minor

PLATES

PLATE I
CHIANG YEE

PLATE 2
PEREGRINO DA CESENA

PLATE 3
ADAM ELSHEIMER

PLATE 4
WILLIAM BLAKE

LONDON INVEN GRAV AND PUB BY EDW.D CALVERT XVII RUSSELL STREET BRIXTON ROAD SEPT.R MDCCCXXXI.

PLATE 5

EDWARD CALVERT

PLATE 6
HANS HOLBEIN

PLATE 7
ALBRECHT ALTDORFER

PLATE 8
JOHN J. A. MURPHY

PLATE 9
JACQUES CALLOT

PLATE 10
REMBRANDT VAN RIJN

PARAD...

PLATE II

CHARLES NICOLAS COCHIN

PLATE 12
THOMAS BEWICK

PLATE 13
FRANCISCO GOYA

PLATE 14
MAX WEBER

poet, Ambrose Philips. The book is now remembered only because of Blake's woodcuts. The wood blocks were not valued by the publisher, for they were not in the conventional and mechanical style of engraved illustrations of the time. So much so, that he felt impelled to insert the following apologetic note:

> The Illustrations of this English Pastoral are by the famous Blake, the illustrator of Young's Night Thoughts and Blair's Grave, who designed and engraved them himself. This is mentioned, as they display less of art than genius, and are much admired by some eminent painters.

Of the twenty existing woodcuts (three were cut by other hands and lost all their quality, and the seventeen cut by Blake escaped recutting only by the intervention of the "eminent painters"), the one entitled *Sabrina's Silvery Flood* (Plate 4) is perhaps the most charming and beautiful. The quintessence of the idyllic and pastoral life is distilled in this tiny woodcut. The mood is serene and peaceful. The composition is basically simple: in the center a stream meanders from background to foreground; the grazing sheep on one side balance the tiny cottage on the other. This block, and several others, were sawed off slightly to fit the page of the printed book. The reproduction here is from a proof of the uncut block—just as Blake made it—which once belonged to John Linnell, Blake's friend and benefactor, and is now in the Lessing J. Rosenwald Collection at the National Gallery of Art in Washington. Blake's woodcuts exemplify most eloquently the idea of much in little. Blake, the poet, has also written one of the most perfect definitions of multum in parvo:

> To see a World in a grain of sand,
> And a Heaven in a wild flower,
> Hold Infinity in the palm of your hand,
> And Eternity in an hour.

A little group of English artists gathered around William Blake in his old age, and were united in their admiration of him and of the pastoral life: Samuel Palmer, John Linnell, George Richmond, and Edward Calvert. Under the inspiration of Blake, Calvert made several copper engravings and lithographs and nine wood engravings. Of these last, *Chamber Idyll* (Plate 5) might well serve as a counterpart to Blake's *Sabrina's Silvery Flood*, for it shows, one might say, the interior of the cottage in Blake's picture. It is one of the most exquisite prints in the history of graphic art. Every detail of the interior is delineated with loving care and inspired craftsmanship—the beams, the casement windows, the implements of the pastoral life. There are glimpses of sheep and cattle bedded for the night, and of the serene starry sky. Here, then, are poesy and romance —romanticism at its very best. Two human beings are the central theme of the picture. Never has the intimacy and tender rapport of man and woman together been suggested with more touching and unaffected simplicity. Calvert has admirably expressed the innocence of sex, wholesome and natural.

There are, however, other aspects to sex, that blind and powerful germinative force in all life. There are, for instance, passion and the frustration of passion, sex coupled with sin, as in the love of Abélard and Héloïse. This aspect is expressed in the woodcut, *Death and the Virgin*, from Hans Holbein's sequence of the *Dance of Death* (Plate 6). A dramatic conflict is revealed in exquisite and literal detail, the conflict in the girl's mind between chastity and passion, between the duties of religion and the pleasures of this world, between the heavenly bridegroom and a handsome and mundane lover. What sweet compelling music does this lover play on his lute, that can so lead her thoughts astray while praying at the altar, or make her forget her vows, if already committed to the vocation of a nun? Death resolves the conflict at its very crisis by snuffing out the candle of life. We shall never know which way she would have turned; we can only speculate on this and other facets of this thought-provoking print. The theme of death was ever present in the mediaeval mind, and many representations exist of the *Danse Macabre* and its procession of grinning skeletons, to remind men and women that death comes to all ranks from pope to peasant. Holbein's sequence, one of the latest in point of time, has a Renaissance setting, and was first published in book form at Lyon in France in 1538. This particular woodcut, as I have observed, also reveals a moral conflict, the idea of sin as a violation of religious precept, in this instance regarding sex. It has been said that the sense of sin was religion's gift to sex—a garnish to add piquancy, as it were, a taste of forbidden fruit, to the common universal urge. It is true that certain religions, notably the Jewish, Christian, and Buddhist, seek to impose ascetic and other worldly values upon man's erring and instinctive impulses. This clash of values has enriched beyond all calculation mankind's emotional, mental, and spiritual heritage.

Thus it happens that the epic *Passion of Jesus Christ* has been a fertile source of inspiration to artists throughout the ages. Of the many examples in miniature, I offer three in distinctive versions showing the response of artists working in different styles and epochs.

The mood of Albrecht Altdorfer's woodcut *Agony in the Garden* (Plate 7) is one of anguish and tribulation. Everything in the picture contributes to the dominant tone: the wild agitated landscape, the tree with drooping branches, the ambiguous shapes, the unearthly light, the whole phantasmagoric collocation of lines and planes. All natural objects are arranged within the frame, only the visionary cloud breaks out of the containing rectangle. The clod-like bodies of the sleeping apostles are contrasted with the tortured figure of the kneeling Christ, to whom the eye is constantly led. One is reminded of Emily Dickinson's poem:

> I like a look of agony
> Because I know it's true,
> Men do not sham convulsion
> Nor simulate a throe.

In its representation of inner conflict likewise mirrored in outward appearance, this print anticipates the modern Expressionist style. The Gothic spirit has a certain affinity with Expressionism; and Altdorfer, working during the period of transition to the Renaissance, still shows considerable Gothic feeling. This set of *The Passion* in forty woodcuts, executed around 1515, is one of the masterpieces of multum in parvo. It is generally assumed that the artist cut his own designs on wood, contrary to the practice of his time. The woodcuts of Holbein's *Dance of Death*, for example, were cut by Hans Lützelberger, an exceptionally fine craftsman. It is obvious that prints executed by the artist himself do have a more convincing autographic quality, although there are exceptions, as with the partnership of Holbein and Lützelberger, where outstanding design and sensitive response have produced masterpieces.

Next, a modern approach. John J. A. Murphy in his personal greeting card of 1920, the wood engraving *Adoration of the Shepherds* (Plate 8), has built up his com-

[45]

position around the theme of radiance. The emotional impact comes largely from the ecstatic emanation of light from the Christ Child and from the imaginative manipulation of black and white in the *mise en scène*, in other words, a purely visual conception. There is little attempt at historical realism. Details are suppressed or altered for unity of effect: all the shepherds have saintly halos, and no animals, except one lamb in the arms of a shepherd, are present. The mood is one of joy and ecstasy at the birth of the Light of the World.

It is a truism that each epoch assumes that its representations of historical events are realistically faithful, whereas actually they are more or less reflections of contemporary attitudes. To us, Callot's rendering of the *Last Supper* (Plate 9) from his small set of *The Passion* of 1624 seems far removed from historical truth; it would seem rather to depict a stately and elegant banquet in the Renaissance or Baroque manner. Callot's contemporaries apparently were not aware of the discrepancy. No doubt, future generations will be saying as much about our excursions into historical verisimilitude. That which continues to be valid through the ages, however, is the effect which a work of art produces, the thoughts and feelings which it inspires in the beholder. And on this score, Callot's tiny etching is rich in overtones and echoes of a bygone age—the Baroque gesture, the Rome of the Counter-Reformation, the in-

cense and lights and pomp of ecclesiastical ritual, the re-
forms of Palestrina, High Mass at Il Gesù, Frescobaldi at
the organ of St. Peter's. Jacques Callot, exponent of the
Baroque or Mannerist style, was also, by reason of his
consummate draftsmanship and technical skill, one of the
greatest masters of etching in miniature.

Rembrandt was a younger contemporary of Callot, yet
his small etching *The Goldsmith* (Plate 10) of 1655 seems
poles apart from Callot's *Last Supper*: it dramatizes individual quest instead of social gesture, inner truth instead of
outward ritual. Even in his religious prints, Rembrandt
interprets the theme in terms of the human heart rather
than of dogma. In this etching, Rembrandt presents an
allegory of the artist as creator, for it is obvious that the
goldsmith could be any sculptor or indeed any artist. The
setting is simple and unpretentious, merely a workshop
with a forge and the usual tools. What is impressive beyond
measure is the intense absorption of the creator in his work.
Rembrandt has not portrayed the conventional idea of the
artist, but rather the simple homely workman, middle-
aged and careworn, who is creating something more beautiful and enduring than himself. This possibly is a more
significant allegory of the artist's vocation than is generally
presented. Rembrandt does not exhibit a mannered ele-
gance of style; his aim is for character and psychological
truth. The composition of *The Goldsmith*, nonetheless, has

great distinction, a perfection of placement, and that rectangular neatness of arrangement later exemplified by his
fellow countryman, Mondrian.

Charles Nicolas Cochin's etching *Parade* (Plate 11) serves
to recall the glamour of aristocratic life during the *Ancien
Régime*. Perhaps its credentials to rank among the supreme
examples of multum in parvo are not without some question, for part of its fascination is due to its rarity and to its
associations. It happens to have been the admission card to
one of Mme de Pompadour's private theatricals in her
apartments at Versailles. The court favorite was in the
habit of putting on such amateur performances, in which
Louis XV and his entourage, including herself, took part.
One can well imagine the enviable distinction that accrued
from presence at such exclusive and madcap parties, and
the intrigue and heartbreak involved in wangling the
coveted invitation. The performance of *Parade* took place
in 1759, and the ticket shows three characters from the
play: the beautiful Isabelle, her lover Léandre, and the valet
Pierrot. The print reproduced came from the artist's own
complete collection of his works; in general such ephemera
are seldom preserved. Charles Nicolas Cochin, the
Younger, whom Diderot called *le premier dessinateur
français*, was an engaging personality, a writer and engraver
of talent, and a man of singular integrity, considering his
role as a favorite at the court of Louis XV.

From the glitter of high life to the prose of lowly life is but a twist in the kaleidoscope of art. Thomas Bewick's wood engraving *Woman Hanging Out Clothes* (Plate 12) might easily have been a page out of "the short and simple annals of the poor." It appeared as a tailpiece to a chapter in *The History of British Birds* by Bewick in 1797. The vignettes, which he cut as a relaxation from the exacting discipline of ornithological illustration, and which he distributed generously throughout his books, are among the most delightful and authentic of all delineations of rural life in England around 1800. They have humor, topical interest, accurate observation, and above all, viability, a sense of life being lived, however humbly, in and beyond the particular scene portrayed. Thomas Bewick spent most of his life in Newcastle as a simple, provincial craftsman, but his drawing won the admiration of Ruskin and Wordsworth, and his technical system of engraving on end-grain blocks decisively affected book illustration for more than half a century.

With the Spaniard, Francisco Goya, we seem to get a foretaste of the psychological complexities of modern life. In his exploration of irrational, subconscious, and often sinister human motivations, for example, and in his passionate awareness of social injustice and the bestiality of war, Goya sees with the eyes of modern man. One of his most expressive and moving creations is a small etching

[49]

entitled *The Prisoner* (Plate 13). Out of the enveloping shadows of a dark cell—depicted with a mastery of chiaroscuro and draftsmanship which would have excited the admiration of Rembrandt—there emerges the monumental figure of a prisoner. He does not seem to be an ordinary criminal who breaks the law without challenging its validity. The inhuman severity of his punishment suggests a more profound or revolutionary intent: either a bitterly ironic reflection on man's inhumanity to man, or else a composite symbol to represent all those who suffer injustice and are persecuted for righteousness' sake. As the severity of his torture endows the prisoner with a certain martyr-like nobility, so the largeness of design in relation to its tiny scale gives it the *cachet* of multum in parvo.

Monumentality of form and conception has always been a challenge to the artist. The ultimate justification for any striving for monumentality lies in symbolic meaning; and every age has its own response to heroic universal utterance. The present era seems to have discovered it in the basic forms and religious content of primitive art. Thus, Max Weber's woodcut, *Mother and Child* (Plate 14) is more than an aesthetically pleasing design of black and white shapes inspired by African carvings: it is a monumental work of art that speaks in signs and symbols. It is Mother and Child writ large—an act of homage to *Magna Genetrix*, the Great Mother, creator and preserver of life.

Many more choice examples of multum in parvo exist and could be cited, not to mention a multitude of borderline cases as far as size and quality are concerned. Postage stamps or bookplates, for example, do not as a rule measure up to the highest test. Granted that a few stamps are well designed and much esteemed (usually for their rarity), it must be said that stamps are purely decorative or functional, and lack emotional overtones. I cannot refrain, however, from exhibiting one handsome example (Plate 15) designed by Rockwell Kent in 1932, because of its unusual associations. It was cut in wood by the artist in an isolated settlement in the Umanak district of Greenland. It happened that the noted German flier, Ernst Udet, was also stationed there in connection with the filming of a motion picture. In his occasional flights to the mainland of Europe, the German ace offered to take along mail which otherwise would have been held over for the infrequent mail boats. It was for this voluntary and unofficial service that Kent designed the stamp, which he printed with red oil paint rubbed on with a hammer. The proceeds from the sale of the stamps were applied toward the building of an assembly and dance hall for the natives.

Prints of miniature size are often collected. There has even been a society of collectors which commissioned such prints. But most miniature prints are merely small in size, lacking concentration, or else they are bravura pieces, such as John Taylor Arms' rendering of a cathedral on less than a square inch of copper, in the same category as the engraving of the Lord's Prayer on a penny.

Realistic portraits of people and landscapes (which are essentially portraits of Nature) do not, as a general rule, provide apt material for much in little. The basic purpose of both is likeness, and true likeness precludes imaginative variation. Specific detail is documentary, referring to the one and not to the many. The only pure landscape which I have cited, Blake's idyllic pastoral, is imaginary and symbolic, not at all realistic.

The idea of much in little is capable of a wider interpretation. I have shown only the quintessence of multum in parvo. But in comparison with an easel painting, even a large-sized print might contain much in little; and so, likewise, an easel painting in comparison with a fresco or *salon* painting, or a tiny carving in comparison with a huge statue. Some Greek coins or Pisanello medals have the necessary qualifications; and likewise, occasionally, a sculptor's first plastic sketch or *bozzetto*, and an architect's first concept or thumbnail sketch of a building. The one quality which all these works possess in common is their meaningfulness, their capacity to kindle the imagination.

The imaginative faculty is one of man's most precious possessions. And never more so than today. Imagination is the doorway, as it were, to our private world, our one

[52]

escape from total regimentation. Yet in every aspect of our material civilization, in the structure of our economy, in our mass communications, and above all in the education of our children, our imaginative capacities are ignored, suppressed, and stultified. We hear the blare of hi-fi, but not the still small voice. We see the billboard, where he who drives may read, but we do not see the blue flower of Novalis. The machine has almost abolished individual enterprise in the crafts and manufactures. The only area where individual initiative is still possible is in the various arts, visual, literary, musical, or religious. Even though not all of us can be artists, we still can participate imaginatively in their achievements. The power of imagination can make artists of us all.

Herein lies the point and moral of this essay : it is a tribute to poetic imagination, and an earnest plea for its cultivation. By *poetic* I do not mean to impose literary conventions upon all the arts. I am using the word *poet* in its true and original sense as *maker* or *creator*. Poetic imagination is that complex of feeling and thinking, of empathy and sympathy, of play-acting with ideas and attitudes, which enables anyone to recapitulate and re-create to some degree the original work of art. It is related to the mimic play instinct of children and animals. Its field is in the fructifying interplay between myth and reality. When directed toward invention instead of re-creation, by drawing upon

[53]

the image-making resources of the subconscious, and when coupled with the techniques of visualization and projection, it becomes creative imagination, the artist's greatest asset. But, as I have said, its greatest scope and value is for the layman, especially in this age of vicarious and collective living. It enables each one of us to establish an individual identity, and to participate in a personal and genuine experience. To the artist, poetic imagination gives depth of meaning; to the layman, the key to another world.

Ralph Waldo Emerson in a gnomic saying summed up the role of art in enriching our lives.

> Art should exhilarate, and throw down the walls of circumstance on every side, awakening in the beholder the same sense of universal relation and power which the work evinced in the artist.

What does this mean? That art should exhilarate is obvious. To throw down the walls of circumstance is to lift us out of the routine of existence, to invite us to exciting adventures of the spirit, to experience new feelings or new ideas, to travel far and near, to every country of the globe, and even into the past. To awaken the sense of universal relation and power is, of course, the height of wisdom and enlightenment. Such are the delights and advantages of the imaginative life and a participation in the arts. Physically, we have but one life to live. But we can live countless lives in imagination.

Designed and printed at the Spiral Press, New York

Plates by the Meriden Gravure Company